A Collection of Inspired Poems

By Alva Williams

Acknowledgments

I dedicate this book to My Lover, My Lord and My Savior, Jesus Christ. He has been my strength, my friend and my defender all of my life. I also dedicate this book to my husband, LeShay Williams, who has always believed in me, since we first met. He makes me feel like there is nothing that I can't do. I love my husband and I thank him for believing in me, trusting me, supporting me, loving me, being my friend and most importantly, for being my Brother in Christ! Now finally, I dedicate this book of poetry to my late sister,

Elizabeth Robinson (Harris), who I love so much! I remember when I first started writing, she was my biggest fan. She would have her friends read my poems; and she eventually became instrumental in my writing poems to help ease the emotional pain of others. She gave me my first credit card, came to my graduations, marriage, came out of town to meet all of my newborns, gave me advice, she made me laugh, made me angry, made me happy and made me proud. The last time we talked it was about God, and that was perfect because she was also my Sister-in-Christ.

I Love you Lou, You're Not Forgotten

To My Readers

My hope for each of you who read this book of poetry is that at least one of my poems will touch your heart. I like to say that my poetry is, "As simple as black and white"
When my poetry is read, my desire is that each person understands what they are reading and take a moment to Reflect on past joys, Embrace love or Receive healing. These poems were written to inspire the heart. Although my poems may not have been written specifically for you, if the God who helped me create this book and who also, designed all of our hearts led you to this book, then each poem that touches your heart was designed with you in mind for this very moment in time!
The richest people have embraced how deeply God loves and adores them; and no one can take this truth from them.
May God's Grace and Mercy keep you always!

With Love, Alva

Oh How She Loved You

By Alva Williams, recited at my sister's funeral "2007"

SHE SPENT HER WHOLE LIFE
DESIRING LOVE
SHE SPENT HER WHOLE LIFE
POURING OUT HER LOVE

TRAVELING TO BOSTON
PENNSYLAVANIA
NORTH CAROLINA AND VIRGINIA
JUST TO SEE YOU

BRUTELY HONEST
YET ALSO KIND
NOT HERSELF
BUT YOU ON HER MIND

EYES THAT SMILED
AND DANCED WITH LAUGHTER
TEARS OF HUMOR
SOON FOLLOWING AFTER

AND OH! HOW SHE LOVED YOU

FINDING TIME TO FIX
PROBLEMS NOT HER OWN
WANTING NO ONE
TO FEEL LEFT ALONE

ALWAYS STRIVING
TO DO HER BEST
AND FROM LOVED ONES
SHE EXPECTED NO LESS

LOVING HER PATIENTS
LIKE THEY WERE HER OWN
AND MOURNING THEIR DEATH
WHEN SOME WERE CALLED HOME

SHE WAS GUILTY
OF SHOWING UP
FOR FUNERALS, GRADUATIONS
THE BIRTH OF A CHILD

OR A FOOTBALL GAME
JUST A FEW
EVENTS
TO NAME

AND OH! HOW SHE LOVED YOU

STAYING IN TOUCH
WITH FAMILY AND FRIENDS
NOT ALLOWING ANY OF HER
RELATIONSHIPS TO END

TO YOU SHE WAS MOTHER, DAUGHTER,
GRANDDAUGHTER, AUNTIE, NIECE, COUSIN A FRIEND
AND SHE LOVED EACH OF YOU
SHE CONSIDERED YOU KIN

SHE GAVE HER LIFE
TO JESUS CHRIST
AND WARNED MOST OF YOU
YOU'D BETTER THINK TWICE

SHE SPENT HER LIFE
DRAWING US ALL TOGETHER
SO PLEASE DON'T HATE AND
DEVOUR EACH OTHER

SHE INVESTED HER LOVE
INTO ALL OF YOU
IT WASN'T JUST FAMILY
SHE LOVED HER FRIENDS TOO

SHE BROUGHT
HER GREAT FAMILY
UNDER THIS ONE ROOF
THE LIFE SHE LIVED
YOU
YOU'RE THE PROOF

REMEMBERED AS ELIZABETH, LITTLE BIT, LIZ OR LOU
WITH HER GREAT BIG HEART.......

AND OH! HOW SHE LOVED YOU

In remembrance of my sister with love

Elizabeth Robinson/Harris

Dedicated mother and nurse

Her life on earth: March 30, 1966 — Friday, January 5, 2007

1 Thessalonians 4:13-18

Now also we would not have you ignorant, brethren, about those who fall asleep [in death], that you may not grieve [for them] as the rest do who have no hope [beyond the grave]. For since we believe that Jesus died and rose again, even so God will also bring with Him through Jesus those who have fallen asleep [in death]. For this we declare to you by the Lord's [own] word, that we who are alive and remain until the coming of the Lord shall in no way precede [into His presence] or have any advantage at all over those who have previously fallen asleep [in Him in death]. For the Lord Himself will descend from heaven with a loud cry of summons, with the shout of an archangel, and with the blast of the trumpet of God. And those who have departed this life in Christ will rise first. Then we, the living ones who remain [on the earth], shall simultaneously be caught up along with [the resurrected dead] in the clouds to meet the Lord in the air; and so always (through the eternity of the eternities) we shall be with the Lord! Therefore comfort and encourage one another with these words. [Amp]

YOU CAN ALWAYS COME HOME

LET ME TAKE YOU BACK
TO THE DAY
WHEN I REFUSED TO SAY
LORD SHOW ME YOUR WAY

YOU SEE I HAD MADE
A TERRIBLE CHOICE
I WOULD NOT HEED
MY MASTER'S VOICE

SO THERE I WAS
OUT ON MY OWN
BUT HE CONTINUED TO SAY
YOU CAN ALWAYS COME HOME

I SAID NO, NO, NO
IT'S TOO LATE FOR ME
GO AHEAD
SET SOMEBODY ELSE FREE

HE SAID I DIDN'T DIE
SO YOU COULD WALK ALONE
I PLEAD WITH YOU
TO COME BACK HOME

I JUST SIGHED
RIGHT BEFORE I CRIED
BECAUSE I KNEW
THAT I WAS LIVING A LIE

YOU SEE I LIVED AS THOUGH
LIFE WAS ALL ABOUT ME
AND I HAD THE POWER
TO SET MYSELF FREE

HE SAID I AM THE TRUTH
I'M NOT A LAIR
AND BRINGING YOU HOME
IS MY HEARTS DESIRE

OH LORD, PLEASE FORGET ABOUT ME
MY LIFE IT'S SO FILTHY
AND THERE'S JUST SO MUCH
I DON'T WANT YOU TO SEE

HE SAID, HA
YOU WERE MINE, WHEN YOU WERE DOING FINE
AND YOU STILL WERE MINE
WHEN YOU FELL BEHIND

YOU'RE NOT THE ONLY ONE
WHO COMMITTED A CRIME
BUT, YOU'VE GOT TO COME HOME
AND STOP WASTING TIME

BUT LORD I'M ALL USED UP
ALL CRIED OUT
MY HEART AND MIND
HAVE BEEN THROWN ABOUT

THE FRIENDS I THOUGHT WERE MINE
STRAIGHT TO THE END
THEY ALL DISAPPEARED
JUST LIKE THE WIND

HE SAID I AM THE BEGINNING
NO I'M NOT THE END
I'LL CLAIM THE ROLE
AS YOUR LONG LOST FRIEND

YOUR MINE
I LOVE YOU AS A MOTHER LOVES HER BABY
AND ALL YOUR MISTAKES
THEY DO NOT FAZE ME

THEN LORD ANSWER ME, WHAT MUST I DO
TO COME HOME AND NEVER LEAVE YOU
I WANT TO LIVE RIGHT GET MY LIFE TOGETHER
AND SERVE YOU FOREVER AND EVER

HE SAID BELIEVE IN MY AUTHORIZATION
FOR YOUR LAVITATION, INNOVATION,
RECONCILIATION, MODIFICATION, NOT TO
MENTION YOUR NEW DIRECTION,
STAYED AFFECTION, NO APPREHENSION

AND IT'S NOT YOU
WHO'S ALL USED UP
IT'S THAT WORD
BUT, BUT, BUT

BUT IM NOT READY
BUT IT'S NOT TIME
I'M WAITING ON YOU
TO FIND A NEW LINE

BELIEVE IN ME
AND UNDERSTAND
MY TRUTH, WILL
MAKE YOU A NEW MAN

I'M HERE WILLING,
READY AND WAITING
FOR YOU TO COME HOME
AND CLAIM YOUR SALVATION

I REACH OUT MY HAND
AS I PLEAD WITH YOU
COME BACK HOME
SO WE CAN START ANEW

BECAUSE
I'M STILL
IN LOVE
WITH YOU!

Jeremiah 29:11-13

For I know the thoughts that I think towards you, saith the Lord, thoughts of peace, and not of evil, to give you an expected end. Then shall ye call upon me, and ye shall go and pray unto me, and I will hearken unto you. And ye shall seek me, and find me, when ye shall search for me with all your heart.

THE DROP OF A TEAR

THE DROP OF A TEAR
THE FALLING OF RAIN
BOTH VERY DIFFERENT
YET SO MUCH THE SAME

BUILT IS A STORM
BUILT IS A THREAT
BUILT IS THE ASSURANCE
OF A FLOOD YET MET

ONE DAY A YOUNG MAN
WENT ASTRAY
SOON HE TOTALLY
LOST HIS WAY

THE DROP OF A TEAR
THE FALLING OF RAIN
HE WONDERS AND WONDERS
WHAT WILL HE GAIN

TURNING AWAY
BUT UNABLE TO ERASE
THE PAIN AND CONFUSION
ETCHED UPON HIS FACE

LIFE IS A WASTE
AND NO ONE CARES
THE STORM ENWRAPS HIM
ALONG WITH HIS FEARS

HE HOLDS HIGH HIS HEAD
AND STICKS OUT HIS CHEST
LOOKS ABROAD
AND SAYS I AM THE BEST

HE LONGS TO SLEEP
HE LONGS TO REST
BUT, HE KNOWS THERE ARE
OTHERS WHO LONG TO BE BEST

HARD COLD, BLACK, SLEEK
THE GUN SCREAMS SHEER
DEFEAT ITS VICTIM IS STILL
FOR HE CAN NOT RETREAT

A SINGLE TEAR
ROLLS DOWN HIS CHEEK
AS HE WEAKLY
STRUGGLES TO SPEAK

HE MUMBLE WORDS
THAT ARE VERY MEEK
FOR HE HAS FELT
TOTAL DEFEAT

SOMEONE KNEELS
CLOSE TO HIS FACE
THEY HEAR HIM MUMBLE
"MY LIFE WAS A WASTE"

THE BLOOD AND MUD
MINGLE WITH RAIN, THERE WAS
NOTHING TO BE GAINED
NOW HE LIES AMIDST HIS FAME

HE DIED NOT BELIEVING
FOR HIM JESUS CAME
HELL IS THE ONLY PRIZE
HE NOW CAN CLAIM

THE DROP OF A TEAR
THE FALLING OF RAIN
PLEASE DON'T CHOOSE
THIS PATH OF PAIN

THE DARKNESS OF HELL
ETERNAL SHAME
KNOWING YOU NEVER
LIVED IN JESUS NAME

THE TEARS AND RAIN
CASCADE DOWN
FALLING AIMLESSLY TO THE GROUND

THE DROP OF A TEAR
THE FALLING OF RAIN
BOTH VERY DIFFERENT
YET SO MUCH THE SAME....

Revelation 21:7-8

He that overcometh shall inherit all things; and I will be his God, and he shall be my son. But the fearful, and unbelieving, and the abominable, and murderers, and whoremongers, and sorcerers, and idolaters, and all liars shall have their part in the lake which burneth with fire and brimstone: which is the second death.

DEAR MOM & DAD

DON'T TREAT ME LIKE
I'M DEAD AND GONE
MY BODY IS DEAD
BUT MY SPIRIT LIVES ON

TO YOU IT MAY SEEM
MY LIFE HAD JUST BEGUN
BUT I'M ALIVE IN HEAVEN
ME! YOUR SON

BEFORE YOU EVEN KNEW
THAT I WOULD BE
GOD ALREADY KNEW
WHAT WOULD HAPPEN TO ME

I'M SORRY THAT I COULDN'T
STAY WITH YOU FOR LONG
BUT HEAVEN IS WHERE
I NOW BELONG

DON'T WORRY
CAUSE JESUS IS HERE WITH ME
AND I TOLD HIM YOU GUYS
TOOK GOOD CARE OF ME

MOM, I WANT YOU AND DAD
TO FORGET SOMETHING FOR ME
THE SMALL LITTLE CHILD
THAT I USED TO BE

HEAVEN IS NOTHING AT ALL
LIKE EARTH
IN HEAVEN MY BODY
NO LONGER HURTS

I NEED YOU TO KNOW
THAT I AM NOT GONE
WHEN MY BODY DIED
MY SPIRIT WAS BORN

DON'T BE SAD BECAUSE
YOU CAN'T TOUCH ME NO MORE
LOVE HAS NO BOUNDS
OF THIS I AM SURE

I HAVE CHANGED FROM THE
CHILD THAT I USED TO BE
NOW PLEASE ACCEPT
THOSE CHANGES IN ME

REJOICE ON THE DAY
THAT I WAS BORN
BECAUSE I'M STILL ALIVE
EVEN THOUGH I AM GONE

MY MEMORY IS ALWAYS
LURKING ABOUT
EMBRACE ME, PLEASE
DON'T SHUT ME OUT

I KNOW SOMETIMES
IT REALLY GETS HARD
BUT THAT'S WHEN YOU
SHOULD TURN TO GOD

SEE, THERE ARE TIMES
WHEN I MISS YOU GUYS TOO
AND JESUS IS WHO
I ALWAYS TALK TO

I COULD GO ON AND ON
SAYING THAT. I'M O.K.
SO THIS IS THE LAST THING
I WANT TO SAY

LOVE MY JESUS
AND LIVE YOUR LIFE
BECAUSE MOM & DAD
EVERYTHING IS ALRIGHT.....

1 Corinthians 15:42-46

So it is with the resurrection of the dead. [The body] that is sown is Perishable and decays, but [the body] that is resurrected is imperishable (immune to decay, immortal). It is sown in dishonor and humiliation; it is raised in honor and glory. It is sown in infirmity and weakness; it is resurrected in strength and endued with power. It is sown a natural (physical) body; it is raised a supernatural (a spiritual) body. [As surely as] there is a physical body, there is also a spiritual body. Thus it is written, The first man Adam became a living being (an individual personality); the last Adam (Christ) became a life-giving Spirit [restoring the dead to life]. But it is not the spiritual life which came first, but the physical and then the spiritual. [Amp]

MAY I COME IN

When I knock

Will you answer

May I come in

May I walk

The halls

Of your mind

Will you

Allow me

To touch old patterns

Old patterns

Engraved in your mind

May I come in

I'll carve images

Of Me

The Living Word

Upon your heart

In your mind

May I come in

My jewel

My poem

My special possession

For you

I make all things new

May I come in

May I travel

the concourse of your heart

May I rearrange the art work

I'll repair the broken porcelain and

shattered crystal of your dreams

May I come in

I'm so excited

I'll hang new pictures

Lay fresh carpet

Repaint the walls

Pure white

May I come in

The strongholds you guard

Let me pull them down

Please I bid you, may I come in

I'll put fresh lilies

In the corners

Of your mind

Will you

Permit me access

To every room

I'll clean the windows

No more residue

Blocking you from Me

I'll be gentle with your heart

Together we'll create a new rhythm

May I come in

Little sheep misunderstood

I am the Good Shepherd

I stand at your door

I love you

The apple of my eye

May I come in........

Revelations 3:19-22

Those whom I [dearly and tenderly] love, I tell their faults and convict and convince and reprove and chasten [I discipline and instruct them]. So be enthusiastic and in earnest and burning with zeal and repent [changing your mind and attitude]. Behold, I stand at the door and knock; if anyone hears and listens to and heeds My voice and opens the door, I will come in to him and will eat with him, and he [will eat] with Me. He who overcomes (is victorious), I will grant him to sit beside Me on My throne, as I Myself overcame (was victorious) and sat down beside My Father on His throne. He who is able to hear, let him listen to and heed what the [Holy] Spirit says to the assemblies (churches). [Amp]

MY BROTHERS

My brothers!
Full of nobility
So strong, so regal
And absolutely free

Free to choose
A life
Of honor
And integrity

Society tries
To dull your purpose
And suggest
You're obsolete

They imply
You're not needed
We have
Technology

Yes technology
And science
Has freed
Society

Freed us of the need
To have
A man
In the home

Freed us of the need
To have
A father
Of our own

Freed us of the need
To have the strength
Of
A man

Freed us of the need
To watch
A boy
Become a man

Society is not free
But you are
Regal
Man

Reclaim
Your post
Because this world
Needs a man

Your not obsolete
Or irrelevant
You're needed more than ever
To do what women can't

Green, White or Black
You have what women lack
The natural inner father who
Can take our children back

Our children need
A woman, and also a man
A home that is complete
God's original plan

Oh my regal brother
Don't you understand
Science can't replace you
Only YOU can be a man!

1 Peter 3:6-9

It was thus that Sarah obeyed Abraham [following his guidance and acknowledging his headship over her by] calling him lord (master, leader, authority). And you are now her true daughters if you do right and let nothing terrify you [not giving way to hysterical fears or letting anxieties unnerve you].

In the same way you married men should live considerately with [your wives], with an intelligent recognition [of the marriage relation], honoring the woman as [physically] the weaker, but [realizing that you both] are joint heirs of the grace (God's unmerited favor) of life, in order that your prayers may not be hindered and cut off. [Otherwise you cannot pray effectively.] Finally, all [of you] should be of one and the same mind (united in spirit), sympathizing [with one another], loving [each other] as brethren [of one household], compassionate and courteous (tenderhearted and humble). Never return evil for evil or insult for insult (scolding, tongue-lashing, berating), but on the contrary blessing [praying for their welfare, happiness, and protection, and truly pitying and loving them]. For know that to this you have been called, that you may yourselves inherit a blessing [from God—that you may obtain a blessing as heirs, bringing welfare and happiness and protection]. [Amp]

DEAR HEART

I THOUGHT LOVE

WAS NOT

TO BE MINE

UNTIL HEAVEN

STRECHED FORTH

HIS HANDS OF GRACE

AND I HEARD

YOUR SPIRIT

SPEAK TO ME OF FOREVER

HOW TIME TRIED

TO CONQUER

THIS PROMISE OF LOVE

STILL A VISION CARVED

INTO MY HEART

THE BEAUTY OF YOUR FACE

LOVE CAME

SO SOFTLY

AS FLOWERS DO BLOOM

NOW I TOUCH

WHAT I THOUGHT

COULD NEVER BE

A HEART THAT SPOKE

FOREVER TO ME

DEAR HEART!

Genesis 29:18-20

And Jacob loved Rachel; and said, I will serve thee seven years for Rachel thy younger daughter And Laban said, it is better that I give her to thee, than that I should give her to another man: abide with me. And Jacob served seven years for Rachel; and they seemed unto him but a few days, for the love he had to her.

I Belong To You

My name is Jesus
I am Holy & True
My love, my bride
I belong to you

Lust after me
Stalk me
Harasses me, my love
I'm yours, I belong to you

Receive my hand
Let me love you,
Hold you,
Shelter you from harm

When your heart is broken
Your world ripped in two
Embrace me, ensue me
I belong to you

Touch me
Handle me
See that I am real
My treasure, I died for you

For God
So loved the world
That He gave His only son
My jewel, I was broken for you

My son, my daughter
I am your salvation
I am your redeemer
I am your friend

Possess me
Claim me
Make me your own
My beloved, I belong to you

John 3:16-17

For God so love the world that he gave his
only begotten Son that whosoever believeth in
Him should not perish but have everlasting life
for God sent not his son into the world
to condemn the world but that the world
through Him might be saved.

I Am Royalty

Who Are You
Telling ME what I
Can't
Be

Honey
I am beautiful
Birth three big boys
And still fine

You! Trying to convince ME
Of who I can't be
Trying to determine
MY destiny

OH!
Baby Please
You have never even seen
Royalty such as me

I am smart
Funny, beautiful
And yes
I am kind

I am patient, tenacious
Poet, author
And, oh yes
Still fine

See no one told you
About my past
They didn't tell you
Where I am really from

I'm from the streets, the hood
A place called Bean town
The liquor store, the mall
Even a cage

Caged like an animal, where can I go
Heavy chain and pad lock
To keep me in
Bars on the windows a ten foot fence

Sounds like a prison
Oh no! That was home
But still! I'm smart beautiful
And Yes, I'm kind

I celebrate my freedom
So don't even THINK
About stepping to me
And trying to telling ME

Who I can't be
Because sweetie
You're looking at
Royalty

I'm an heir…yes, Royalty
Destined from birth
To dominate
Defying your minds reality

Unable to expire
I'm immortal
With my tongue
I enforce change

I rule my life
my will a dynasty
I decide
who I will be

God said, "I put before you
Life and death, now choose"
God suggested I choose life
But He told ME to choose

A worthy opponent
I expect to win
I'm unstoppable, undefeated
MY destiny; I hold in my hands

Only a King
can understand me
because I too
Am Royalty…..

Romans 8:14-18

For as many as are led by the Spirit of God they are the sons of God. For ye have not received the spirit of bondage again to fear; but ye have received the spirit of adoption whereby we cry Abba, Father. The Spirit itself beareth witness with our spirit that we are the children of God: And if children, then heirs; heirs of God, And joint-heirs with Christ; if so be that we suffer with Him that we may be also glorified together. For I reckon that the sufferings of this present time are not worthy to be compared with the glory which shall be revealed in us.

I AM HOLY SPIRIT

GENESIS CHAPTER
ONE
AND VERSE 2
READS

THE SPIRIT OF GOD
WAS HOVERING OVER THE WATER
IT WAS I HOLY SPIRIT
NOT GOD THE FATHER

I AM THE ONE
SENT FROM UP ABOVE
BEFORE THIS WORLD
I ALREADY WAS

BEFORE GOD CREATED
THE HUMAN LIFE
HE SPOKE TO ME
LET THERE BE LIGHT

SEE THE FATHER AND SON
THEY ARE ONE
SO IF EITHER ONE SPEAKS
I GET THE JOB DONE

TOGETHER WE ARE
THE TRINITY
WE OPERATE IN UNITY
TO SET MEN FREE

BUT SO MANY PEOPLE THINK
THAT I DON'T EXIST
SOMETIMES I'M REFERRED
TO AS SIMPLY "IT"

SO HEAR ME NOW
LISTEN TO WHAT I SAY
IF YOU TELL ME TO GO
I'LL WALK AWAY

I WON'T CURSE YOUR NAME
SPIT ON YOUR FEET
I'LL FIND ANOTHER SAINT
WHO WILL WELCOME ME

FOR I AM THE ONE
WHO HELPS YOU TO PRAY
I ALREADY KNOW
WHAT YOU NEED TO SAY

AND I WANT
YOU TO KNOW
ANOTHER THING
ABOUT ME

I'M IN THE WIND
AND THE FIRE
I ANOINT YOU TO LIFT
JESUS HIGHER

WHEN I CAME UPON JESUS
AS THE DOVE
I GAVE HIM POWER
AND HE KNEW WHO I WAS

HE THEN HEALED THE SICK
CURED THE BLIND
AND TURNED PLAIN WATER
INTO THE BEST OF WINE

BEFORE HE LEFT
HE MADE A PROMISE TO YOU
GREATER THINGS THAN THESE
SHALL YOU DO

SO DON'T FLINCH WHEN YOU HEAR
SOMEONE'S ANOINTED TO HEAL
FIND FAITH, BECAUSE MY
POWERS REAL

I CAN TAKE A POOR MAN
AND MAKE HIM A KING
OR DESTROY A WHOLE
NATION OF THE ENEMY

I'M SOFT AND GENTLE
AS THE DOVE
AND POWERFUL LIKE A LIONESS
DEFENDING HER CUB

I CAN HURT, I CAN CRY
OH YES, I CAN FEEL
SO PLEASE, UNDERSTAND
THAT MY FEELINGS ARE REAL

DON'T TAKE ME FOR GRANTED
I'M FAR FROM DEAD
AND BY THE WAY
THIS TOO SHOULD BE SAID

PRAISE FATHER, SON
AND HOLY SPIRIT
I'LL REPEAT THAT AGAIN
IN CASE YOU DIDN'T HEAR IT

PRAISE FATHER, SON
AND HOLY SPIRIT
WE ARE ONE, YET THREE
AND REFERRED TO AS HE
SO PLEASE DON'T DIMINISH ME

FOR I AM NOT AN "IT"
AND I AM NOT A THING
GOD SAYS THAT I'M
A PART OF HIM

NOW TAKE HEED, DO NOT
BLASPHEME AGAINST ME
BECAUSE GOD WON'T
EXCUSE YOU FOR THAT DEED

SEE GOD LOVES ME
AND HE LOVES YOU TOO
SO TOGETHER
GREATER THINGS
SHALL WE DO

FOR I AM LOVE, I AM JOY
I AM POWER AND WIT
I AM GOD
I AM HOLY SPIRIT

Ephesians 4:29-32

Let no corrupt communication proceed out of your mouth but that which is good to the use of edifying that it may minister grace unto the hearers and grieve not the Holy Spirit of God whereby ye are sealed unto the day of redemption. Let all bitterness, and wrath, and anger, and clamour, and evil speaking be put away from you, with all malice and be ye kind one to another, tenderhearted, forgiving one another, even as God for Christ's sake Hath forgiven you.

BLACK AGAINST BLACK

It is I your Father
Eternity
It seems that someone's
Been addressing Me

About
Beauty
Being a color
Or a shade

I've given it time
But this attitude
Does not
Seem to fade

So I've taken this moment
And stepped out of time
To let you know
What is on My mind

I'm trying to figure out
Which one of you
Posses the gift
To reproduce

Maybe it's just Me
But I don't remember
You having the gift
To choose someone's gender

Let's go back
And review A & B
It seems those gifts are
Reserved for Me

It is the Lord
Your God
Who chooses
The color of man

So
Please
Help Me
To understand

Why are words
Of distaste
Attacking
My ears

I hear yellow is beautiful
Brown is good
Black is alright
But dark, dark, black

Oh, we'd rather not
Comment on that
You say:
"I don't think like that,"

But I say,
"I have eyes like superman
I can see into the heart
Of every man"

Your forefathers were
As black as tar
You'd better recognize
Just who you are

And my heart cries
For the lighter man too
I know of the scars
Persecution left you

You've been locked in a cage
Titled "your no better than me,"
But I say come forth,
I set you free

Can anyone stand
Before the living God
And say my color is
The best by far

I am not addressing
The issue of white and black
I'm addressing the attack
Of black against black

In My word
It is written
A house that is divided
Can not stand

How is
your house
Regal
black man

Returning to the lesson
Of A & B
When you attack anyone
You're attacking Me

Keep in mind
That you've never seen Me
So how can you define
True beauty

Can anyone stand
Before the living God
And say my color is
The best by far

It was not you who chooses
The color for a man
It is I your God
The great I AM

Regardless of the shade
Of black you see
All men were made
In the image of Me

You are a blessed people
With many shades of color
I ask you to love
And exalt each other

So when you meet someone
Colored different than you
Remember that I
Made them perfect too...

Genesis 1:27-28

So God created man in His own image, in the image of God created He him; male and female created He them. And God blessed them, and God said unto them, be fruitful, and multiply, and replenish the earth, and subdue it: and have dominion over the fish of the sea, and over the fowl of the air, and over every living thing that moveth upon the earth

SPECIAL MOTHER

You could have quit
Said this is it
I'm walking
out the door

But only you knew
What brought you through
A simple
"I Yove you"

Remember when you wanted to rest
The house was in a mess
Your patience was put to the test
And burdens lay on your chest

But only you knew
What brought you through
Those bright trusting eyes
Depending on you

Remember that day you sighed
And then that night you cried
Fell off to sleep wondering
Why, why, why

But only you knew
What brought you through
The quiet voice of God
Saying "I'm here for you"

Remember your funds were spent
A dime seemed heaven sent
And your mind kept wondering
Over and over where your money went

But only you knew
What brought you through
A promise from God
"I'll never leave you"

If only someone knew
What brought you through
They would understand why
I LOVE YOU!

John 19:25-27

Now there stood by the cross of Jesus his mother, and his mother's sister, Mary the wife of Cleophas, and Mary Magdalene. When Jesus therefore saw his mother, and the disciple standing by, whom he loved, he saith unto his mother, Woman, behold thy son. Then saith He to the disciple, behold thy mother. And from that hour that disciple took her unto his own home.

OUR LOVE

Touch my hands
My lips
My face
Of my heart
Take a taste

Whisper your love
To the evening breeze
And I'll gather each word
From the jubilant trees

And when our love
Can be no more
I'll send it to drift
Out with the shore

I'll tell my heart
That it is free
But our love
Will own the sea!

Song of Solomon 8:7

Many waters cannot quench love, neither can the floods drown it: If a man would give all the substance of his house for love, it would utterly be neglected.

OPEN THE DOOR

YOU TOLD ME YOU WERE TIRED
YOU CRIED PLEASE SET ME FREE
BUT WHEN I PICKED YOU UP
YOU TURNED AWAY FROM ME

WHEN YOU WERE DOWN AND OUT
MY NAME I HEARD YOU SHOUT
BUT WHEN I GAVE YOU GRACE
YOU PRAYED TO ME IN DOUBT

YOU CAME INTO MY HOUSE
YOU GATHERED WITH MY SAINTS
BUT WHEN IT CAME TIME TO WORK
YOU HAD TO CONTEMPLATE

YOU SAID THAT YOU WERE MINE
YOU SAID THAT I WAS YOURS
BUT WHY IS IT THAT WHEN I KNOCKED
YOU ONLY CRACKED THE DOOR

YOU SAID YOU WERE IN PAIN
YOU CRIED OUT IN MY NAME
BUT WHEN I KNOCKED A SECOND TIME
YOU THEN THREW ON THE CHAIN

YOU HASTILY IMPLORED
LORD I WILL FOLLOW THEE
BUT WHEN I KNOCKED A THIRD TIME
YOU SLAMMED THE DOOR ON ME

I HEARD A CLICKING SOUND
AS YOU LOCKED THE DOOR
AND IT WAS AT THAT MOMENT WHEN
YOUR PRAYERS I HEARD NO MORE

Matthew 22:37-40

Jesus said unto him, Thou shalt love the Lord thy God with all thy heart, and with all thy soul, and with all thy mind. This is the first and great commandment. And the second is like unto it, Thou shalt love thy neighbour as thyself. On these two commandments hang all the law and the prophets.

ALIVE!

I'M ALIVE, I'M ALIVE
YES I LIVE
LET ME TELL YA'LL ABOUT IT
HERE IT IS

BIG, BAD SATAN
THOUGHT THAT I WAS DEAD
LET ME TELL YA'LL WHAT
THOSE DEMONS SAID

"OUR MASTER KILLED CHRIST
HE'S ALL BOUND UP
HE'S DEAD I TELL YOU!"
THEN I HEARD
"YUP-YUP!"

I DIDN'T TWINKLE MY NOSE
OR
CLICK MY FEET
I JUST SAID SATAN
YOU'D BEST RETREAT

I GATHERED ALL OF MY SAINTS
FROM HERE AND THERE
THEN I SAID TO SATAN
"EXCUSE ME BRO

ONE FALLEN ANGEL
CAN'T STOP MY SHOW
SO LONG LOSER
WE'VE GOT TO GO"

HE SAID, "JESUS YOUR VICTORY
WILL NOT LAST"
BUT YA BETTER BELIEVE
HE LET US PASS

BEFORE I LEFT
I TURNED TO YELL BACK
"LU...YOU HAD A GREAT HOME
TOO BAD
YA DIDN'T KNOW HOW TO ACT

HE THREW UP HIS HANDS
THEN ROLLED HIS EYES
AS I GAVE A HAUGHTY GRIN
AND A QUICK
BYE-BYE

SO NOW! I REIGN!
BUT HERE'S FOOD FOR THOUGHT
THERE'S STILL A WAR
THAT'S GOT TO BE FOUGHT

I NEED YOU
TO REACH OTHERS
I CAN LOVE
AND ADORE

YOU'VE BEEN GIVEN
THE VICTORY
NOW LEAD SOMEONE ELSE
FROM CAPTIVITY

AND PLEASE DON'T CHOOSE
TO MUMBLE AND GRUMBLE
BECAUSE YOU MIGHT CAUSE
SOMEDOBY ELSE TO STUMBLE

JUST PICK UP YOUR CROSS
DUST IT OFF
PROVE TO ME
MY DEATH WAS NOT A LOSS

I STOOD FOR YOU
NOW STAND FOR ME
MAKE ME NUMBER ONE
ON YOUR ITINARY

YOU ARE THE SALT
OF THIS WORLD
DON'T DIMINISH
STAY IN THE FIGHT

I DIED TO EMPOWER YOU
SO REMEMBER
GREATER WORKS THAN THESE
SHALL YOU DO

I NEVER INTENDED
FOR YOU TO WALK ALONE
I'M HERE SEATED
ON THE THRONE

I NEVER SLEEP
NOR DO I SLUMBER
MY ANGELS FIGHT TOO
MASSIVE IS THEIR NUMBER

SO DON'T LISTEN TO DEVIL
YOU'RE NOT ALONE
BECAUSE
I'M — NOT — DEAD
………… **I LIVE**

Revelation 1:13-18

And in the midst of the lampstands I saw someone like the Son of Man, dressed in a robe reaching to His feet, and with a golden sash wrapped around His chest. His head and His hair were white like white wool, [glistening white] like snow; and His [all-seeing] eyes were [flashing] like a flame of fire [piercing into my being]. His feet were like burnished [white-hot] bronze, refined in a furnace, and His voice was [powerful] like the sound of many waters. In His right hand He held seven stars, and from His mouth came a sharp two-edged sword [of judgment]; and His face [reflecting His majesty and the Shekinah glory] was like the sun shining in [all] its power [at midday]. When I saw Him, I fell at His feet as though dead. And He placed His right hand on me and said, "Do not be afraid; I am the First and the Last [absolute Deity, the Son of God], and the Ever-living One [living in and beyond all time and space]. I died, but see, I am alive forevermore, and I have the keys of [absolute control and victory over] death and of Hades (the realm of the dead). [Amp]

My Dearest Love

If I could brandish

My heart to thee

Genuine love

Is what you'd see

If the fowl could sing

Of how I feel

You would hear them chirp

My love is real

If a dove could coo

The melody of my heart

The rhythm would span

From smooth to sharp

I gaze at the skies
Infinite blue
And I pray our love
Will be infinite too

I pray our words
Will always be true
The love strong
Through and through

If sometimes my love
Reminds you of the sun
Coming up and going down
Remember the sun never touches the ground

Remember the sun

Never truly sets

And my love has been shining

Since the day we met

Remember the sun

Keeps burning bright

Even when the day

Is masked by night

So remember my dearest

And truest love

My love is

And always was……….!

Esther 2:17-18

And the king loved Esther above all the women, and she obtained grace and favour in his sight more than all the virgins; so that he set the royal crown upon her head, and made her queen instead of Vashti. Then the king made a great feast unto all his princes and his servants, even Esther's feast; and he made a release to the provinces, and gave gifts, according to the state of the king.

My Lover

My Lover, My Lord, My King
Whisper your love in my ear

I remember your touch
The scent of fresh lilies

My Lord has need of me
I must meet my Love

My Love longs for my touch, my worship
I must go to Him

Be quiet
for my Love is near

I hear His voice, in the distance, calling to me
The sound of many waters, my heart races

My Lover desires my worship
His Words are sweet like honey

I hunger for my Lover
I ache for His embrace

My Lover, caress me again
I abandon my will to you, my love and my lord

Hold me, My Love
I am yours

Carry me away
My Fortress, My Lord

I am yoked to my Lover
My Lover is yoked to me

My beautiful, handsome Love
May I touch you, my Redeemer

I kiss my Lovers neck, His hands
I rest my head on His holy feet

My Lover kneels down
and runs His hands through my hair

He lifts my head from His feet,
as nail scared hands hold my face to His

Our eyes entwine, He smiles at me
His love for me emanates from His beautiful eyes

My lover gently caresses, the tears staining My face
as I softly whisper to my Love

"My Lord Jesus, I love you…so much"
I am my Lover's, And He is mine

Luke 7:37-43

And behold, a woman in the city, which was a sinner, when she knew that Jesus sat at meat in the Pharisee's house, brought an alabaster box of ointment. And stood at His feet behind Him weeping, and began to wash His feet with tears, and did wipe them with the hairs of her head, and kissed His feet, and anointed them with the ointment. Now when the Pharisee which had bidden Him saw it, he spake within himself, saying, This man, if he were a prophet, would have known who and what manner of woman this is that toucheth Him: for she is a sinner. And Jesus answering said unto him, Simon, I have somewhat to say unto thee. And he saith, Master, say on. There was a certain creditor which had two debtors: the one ought five hundred pence, and the other fifty. And when they had nothing to pay, he frankly forgave them both. Tell me therefore, which of them will love him most? Simon answered and said, I suppose that he, to whom he forgave most. And he said unto him, Thou hast rightly judged.

A TRUE FRIEND

IF SOMEONE ASKED
WHAT IS A FRIEND
THIS IS HOW
MY STORY WOULD BEGIN

A FRIEND IS SOMEONE
JUST LIKE YOU
DEPENDABLE, KIND
HONEST AND TRUE

SOMEONE WHO ALWAYS
SEEMS TO CARE
THEY ALWAYS STEP IN
WHEN NO ONE ELSE IS THERE

A FRIEND IS SOMEONE
WHO CAN PICK YOU UP
WHEN YOUR HEART
FALLS IN A RUT

A FRIEND WILL HELP YOU
OVERCOME PAIN
WHEN THERE IS NOTHING
FOR THAT FRIEND TO GAIN

A FRIEND IN YOU
IS WHAT I HAVE FOUND
YOU HELPED ME LAUGH
WHEN I WANTED TO FROWN

YOUR KIND UNDERSTANDING
IS WORTH A LOT
YOUR GENEROSITY
STRAIGHT FROM THE HEART

I WAS BLESSED WHEN GOD
MADE A FRIEND LIKE YOU
I HOPE MY FRIENDSHIP
IS JUST AS TRUE

SO AS MY STORY
COMES TO AN END
PLEASE UNDERSTAND
THAT YOU ARE MY FRIEND

I HOPE THAT YOU SEE
WHAT YOU ARE TO ME
UNDENIABLE YOU ARE
A TRUE FRIEND INDEED

1 Samuel 18:1-4

When David had finished speaking to Saul, the soul of Jonathan was knit with the soul of David, and Jonathan loved him as his own life. Saul took David that day and would not let him return to his father's house. Then Jonathan made a covenant with David, because he loved him as his own life. And Jonathan stripped himself of the robe that was on him and gave it to David, and his armor; even his sword, His bow, and his girdle.

Choose To Be A Woman

Time won't still
his steady pace
so choose how
you'll run this race

Choose to be a woman
having power and pride
with strength unspoken
yet growing inside

Choose to be a woman
who fights to excel
and in all things
I'm sure you'll do well

Choose to be a woman
with respect and dignity
and all your expectations
will surely come to be

Choose to be a woman
who wants only the best
and God will hand you
all of the rest

Choose to be a woman
who's responsible for
the temple God gave you
and so much more

Choose to be a woman
who's honest and true
and God will always
be there for you

Choose to be a woman
who is supreme
and God will grant
all of your dreams....

Proverbs 31:30-31

Charm and grace are deceptive, and beauty is vain
{because it is not lasting}, but a woman who reverently
And worshipfully fears the Lord, she shall be praised!
Give her of the fruit of her hands, and let her own works
praise her in the gates (of the city}! [Amp]

GOD'S BIBLE ON THE SHELF

RUN SISSY, RUN
OUR MASTER GOT A GUN
HIS ANGER IS HIGH
HE SAY WE GONNA DIE

BUT WHY BIG MARTHA
WHAT DIDN'T WE DO
WE PICKED ALL THE COTTON
AND CLEANED HIS HOUSE TOO

IT'S NOT WHAT WE DIDN'T DO
IT'S WHAT WE HAVE DONE
NOW THE MASTER WANNA SHOOT US
SO RUN, SISSY RUN

I WILL NOT RUN
I HAVE DONE NO WRONG
JESUS CHRIST BE MY STRENGTH
IN HIM, I IS STRONG

OH PLEASE, SISSY RUN
MASTER KNOW WHAT WE DONE
HE SAY HIS BIBLE BEEN READ
NOW HE GONNA SHOOT US DEAD

WHY BIG MARTHA
CAUSE I KNOW HOW TO READ
I'M NEVER GONNA STOP
WHY SHOULD I LEAVE

YA, I READ HIS OLE BIBLE
AND IT'S NOT JUST HIS
THAT BIBLE SAY THROUGH
JESUS CHRIST WE ALL CAN LIVE

THE MASTER, HE'S GREEDY
HE WANT THE BIBLE FOR HISSELF
AND HE NEVER EVEN READ IT
HE JUST KEEP IT ON HIS SHELF

LIKE I SAY BEFORE
I'M NEVER GONNA STOP
I'M GONNA READ AND READ
EVEN IF I GET SHOT

OH SISSY, THAT BIBLE
IT DONE GON TO YOUR HEAD
IF WE DON'T RUN NOW
WE BOTH GON BE DEAD

DON'T YOU WORRY NONE BIG MARTHA

WE GON BE JUST FINE

JESUS BE OR STRENGTH

WE AIN'T GON DIE

SISSY I HEAR HIM

HE RIGHT AT THE DOOR

I'LL HIDE IN THE CORNER

YOU PLAY SLEEP ON THE FLOOR

PRAY BIG MARTHA

PRAY REAL HARD

PRAY HIS CONFUSION

PRAY TO OUR GOD

WAKE UP RIGHT NOW

STAND ON YOUR FEET

YOU'RE A LAZY LITTLE GIRL

ALL YOU EVER DO IS SLEEP

I LEFT WORD THAT I WAS COMING

OVER HERE AND OVER THERE

I HOPED BOTH OF YOU

WOULD HAVE RUN AWAY IN FEAR

SEE I KNOW WHAT YOU DID

YET I'M GONNA LET YOU LIVE

BUT YOU BEST REMEMBER

WHO YOUR MASTER IS

OH YES WE KNOW

WHO OUR MASTER IS

AND WE GIVE HIM PRAISE

FOR ALLOWING US TO LIVE!

SEE THE MASTER WE SERVE

IS A POWERFUL MAN

AND IT'S ON HIS STRENGTH

THAT WE WILL ALWAYS STAND

OUR CONCEITED MASTER

SMILED THINKIN BOUT HISSELF

BUT SISSY WAS TALKIN BOUT

"GOD'S BIBLE ON THE SHELF"

Romans 8:35-39

Who shall separate us from the love of Christ? Shall tribulation, Or distress, or persecution, or famine, or nakedness, or peril, or sword? As it is written, for thy sake we are killed all the day long; we are accounted as sheep for the slaughter. Nay, in all these things we are more than conquerors through Him that loved us for I am persuaded that neither death, nor life, nor angels, nor principalities, nor powers nor things present, nor things to come nor height, nor depth, nor any other creature shall be able to separate us from the love of God which is in Christ Jesus our Lord

A LIE

A LIE
IS A CRY
IN THE NIGHT

A LIE
IS THE TRUTH
HIDDEN FROM SIGHT

A LIE IS SIMPLY
CAMOUFLAGED
REJOICING IN THE NIGHT

THE TRUTH BECOMES
DISTORTED
IN THE SHIMMERING LIGHT

A LIE IS SO SIMPLE
AND FUNNY TO YOU
UNTIL LIE'S FANGS GREW AND GREW

A LIE IS EASY TO SPOUT
UNTIL LIE'S CLAWS
START STICKING OUT

A LIE
IS A TOOL
TO MAKE THINGS RIGHT

UNTIL LIE
LOSES
HIS GROWING MIGHT

THEN LIE
BECOMES
FEBBLE AND WEAK

BECAUSE LIE
WILL RUN
OUT OF WORDS TO SPEAK

BUT A LIE
ISN'T
HARD TO FEED

UNTIL LIE
STARTS FEELING GREED
THEN THE LIAR WILL BLEED........

Proverbs 14:5-8

A faithful witness will not lie: but a false witness will utter lies. A scorner seeketh wisdom, and findeth it not: but knowledge is easy unto him that understandeth. Go from the presence of a foolish man, when thou perceivest not in him the lips of knowledge.

EMBRACE

You took vows
Standing face to face

Then gave each other
Your first embrace

Now embrace the love
You both will give

Embrace the life
You both will live

Embrace the strength
You both will share

Embrace the number
Of each passing year

Embrace the present
Future and past

Then surely
Your love will last

Embrace!

Matthew 19:4-6

And He answered and said unto them, Have ye not read, that He which made them at the beginning made them male and female, and said, for this cause shall a man leave father and mother, and shall cleave to his wife: and they two shall be one flesh? Wherefore they are no more two, but one flesh. What therefore God hath joined together, let not man put asunder.

MY SON

My heart was bound
To you my son
When your life
Had just begun

When first I held you
In my arms
You dazzled me
With all your charm

The day you gave
Your very first smile
I knew you were
A special child

My love for you
Can never grow cold
That love only flourished
As you grew old

As the winds of change
Took hold of your life
I prayed for you
Throughout the night

I can't watch you
Stumble and stagger about
Leaving you to find
Your own way out

I won't turn my back
And close my eyes
Because one day
You will ask me why

You have my essence
You're a part of my soul
I wouldn't trade you
For hills of gold

My hands are outstretched
My arms opened wide
Waiting for you
To put down your pride

Please try
To understand this
You receiving Godly wisdom
Is my greatest wish

Success and victory
I want to incite
within you today
To propel your life

So please keep in mind
When all else fails
Your Mother's love
Will prevail!

2 Kings 4:27-37

And when she came to the man of God to the hill, she caught him by the feet: but Gehazi came near to thrust her away. And the man of God said, let her alone; for her soul is vexed within her: and the Lord hath hid it from me, and hath not told me. Then she said, did I desire a son of my lord? Did I not say, do not deceive me? Then he said to Gehazi, gird up thy lions, and take my staff in thine hand and go thy way: if thou meet any man, salute him not; and if any salute thee, answer him not again: and lay my staff upon the face of the child. And the mother of the child said, as the Lord liveth, and as thy soul liveth, I will not leave thee. And he arose, and followed her. And Gehazi passed on before them, and laid the staff upon the face of the child; but there was neither voice, nor hearing. Wherefore he went again to meet him, and told him, saying, The child is not awaked. And when Elisha was come into the house, behold, the child was dead, and laid upon his bed. He went in therefore, and shut the door upon them twain, and prayed unto the Lord. And he went up, and lay upon the child, and put his mouth upon his mouth, and his eyes upon his eyes, and his hands upon his hands: and he stretched himself upon the child; and the flesh of the child waxed warm. Then he returned, and walked in the house to and fro; and went up, and stretched himself upon him: and the child sneezed seven times, and the child opened his eyes. And he called Gehazi, and said, call this Shunammite. So he called her. And when she was come in unto him, he said, Take up thy son. Then she went in, and fell at his feet, and bowed herself to the Ground, and took up her son, and went out.

I Got Too Much Class

Wardrobe old
Money moving slow
Debt too high
Credit too low

Everybody got jokes
Everybody wanna laugh
But I won't respond
I got too much class

Thinking I'll agree
With your sorry line
"OH GOD!
I'm running out of time"

Sucker punched in the gut
That boy is slick
HEY SATAN!
I'm not gonna quit
I'm not gonna die

So
HONEY
you wipe
YOUR
weepin eye!

Who are **YOU**
Telling **ME**
What I can't be
Two words
I'm Royalty

Resurrecting **MY** sins
From out the past
OH PLEASE!
I got too much class

I have the heart of God
I love the Body of Christ
But unlike you
I can't stand strife

Please understand
Or get a clue
This poem
It's not about you

It's for that punk
That big fat liar
You know.......
The wanna be messiah

When God created man
He had a wonderful dream
The church
Working as a team

Then here come
the devil
With his age old game
His schemes
There all the same

Pitting him against her
And her against him
My patience....
Ya!
It's wearin thin

It's not about us
It's all about
Him
Praise God!
We're all gonna win

So when you're picked
To be harassed
Just laugh and say
I baby too much class

Hebrews 13:1-3

Let LOVE for your fellow believers continue and be a fixed practice with you (never let it fail). Do not forget or neglect or refuse to extend hospitality to Strangers (in the brotherhood—being friendly, cordial, and gracious, sharing the comforts of your home and doing your part generously), for though it some have entertained angels without knowing it. Remember those who are in prison as if you were their fellow prisoner, and those who are ill-treated, since you also are liable to bodily sufferings.
[Amp]

THIS COUPLE IS BLESSED
Miscarriage does not define you

The eyes of Heaven
Slept nor slumbered
As My angels
Looked at Me in wonder

I saw the questions
In their eyes
But none dared
To ask Me, "Why"

"Why", asked eyes
Of different hue
Have you allowed
This pain upon You

Their diligent gaze
Upon Me on My throne
Watched My eyes close
As I let out a moan

I moaned at what
I knew my enemy had done
He ruthlessly attacked
My cherished ones

He attacked his vision
He attacked her dream
He cried, "The Word
Is not what it seems!"

As I spoke to My attending
Angels and cherubim
Two heavenly beings
Bowed down at My throne

They cried, "Holy, holy, holy
Is who You are
Lord we bring good news
From afar

The Man, The Woman
They are both fine
And they've declared
Satan has crossed the line

Boldly they proclaim
That You Lord, are true
And the devil a lair
Through and through

Most High God
King of Kings
The devil has not
Stolen their dreams

Listen carefully!
For El Shaddai speaks
The One who made Himself
Humble and Meek

Go tell the husband
Minister this to his wife
My enemy will pay
For taking this life

All Heaven roared with
Unrestrained glee
As El Shaddai declared
What would and wouldn't be

Then declared Jesus
This issue's at rest
And He loudly proclaimed
This couple is blessed!

Revelation 12:7-11

And there was war in heaven: Michael and his angels fought against the dragon; and the dragon fought and his angels, and prevailed not; neither was their place found any more in heaven. And the great dragon was cast out, that old serpent, called the devil, and Satan, which deceiveth the whole world: he was cast out into the earth, and his angels were cast out with him. And I heard a loud voice saying in heaven, Now is come salvation, and strength, and the kingdom of our God, and the power of his Christ: for the accuser of our brethren is cast down, which accused them before our God day and night. And they overcame him by the blood of the Lamb, and by the word of their testimony; and they loved not their lives unto the death.

THERE'S NO ME, WITHOUT YOU

You have a heart
So tender and true
I can't see me
Without you

Words couldn't capture
This special love
It simply exists
Just because

If I could freeze
A moment in time
It would be when
You first became mine

The words were unspoken
But the feeling was true
That's how I knew
I also belonged to you

You became my husband
I became your wife
We vowed to be together
For the rest of our life

Let's make our life
A beautiful blend
So that we can be
Each others friend

And when I've come
To the end of my road
This is the story
That I want to be told

My love was soft
Tender and true
There never was a me
Without you!

Ecclesiastes 4:9-12

Two are better than one, because they have a good (more satisfying) reward for their labor; For if they fall, the one will lift up his fellow. But woe to him who is alone when he falls and has not another to lift him up! Again, if two lie down together, then they have warmth; but how can one be warm alone? And though a man might prevail against him who is alone, two will withstand him. A threefold cord is not quickly broken.

THE WORSHIPER

HANDS UP LIFTED
SURRENDERED TO GOD
CRY AFTER CRY
LORD TAKE MY ALL

LORD HERE AM I
I'LL STAND IN THE GAP
LORD HEAR AM I
I WON'T TURN BACK

THE WORSHIPER IS
UNCOMMON
UNCOMLEY
BUT FREE

THE WORSHIPER
LUSTS
AFTER
GOD'S GLORY

SPIRIT AND FLESH
EVERYTHING EXPOSED
THE WORSHIPER MUST TRAVEL
THIS PATH ALONE

THE WORSHIPER
IS EMPTY
YET ALSO
FULL

THEY CAN NOT LIVE
THEY MUST DIE
GOD THE ONLY APPLE
OF THE WORSHIPER'S EYE

THE WORSHIPER
IS NOT PERFECT
UNBLEMISED
AND CLEAN

THE WORSHIPER
IS HUMBLE
COVERED
IN BLOOD

THE WORSHIPER
IS YOKED
TO JESUS
GOD'S SON

THE WORSHIPER WILL CRY
NO WORDS TO SPEAK
UNSPEAKABLE JOY
IS WHY THEY WEEP

THE WORSHIPER IS STRONG
THEY KNOW WHAT TO DO
THE WORSHIPER WILL CRY
OUT TO GOD FOR YOU

SEND THE WORSHIPER
THEN THE SWORD
FOR THE BATTLE'S NOT YOURS
IT BELONGS TO THE LORD!

THE WORSHIPER……..

1 Chronicles 16:24-29

Sing unto the LORD, all the earth; shew forth from day to day His salvation. Declare His glory among the heathen; His marvelous works among the nations. For great is the LORD, and greatly to be praised: He also is to be feared above all gods. For all the gods of the people are idols: but the LORD made the heavens. Glory and honour are in His presence; strength and gladness are in His place. Give unto the LORD the glory due unto His name: bring an offering, and come before Him: worship the LORD in the beauty of holiness

THE SECRET

I have a secret
Nobody may know

I have a secret
Though it probably shows

Can't keep this secret
If I try I'll explode

I'm in love
Please let me sing out loud

I'm in love
I'm all gooey inside

I'm in love
I need to dance and shout

I'm in love, Oh Lord
I'm walking on air

I'm in love
With the king of kings

I'm in love
With the Great I AM

I'm in love
With His mercy and grace

I'm in love
I seek my Saviors face

I'm in love
With His soft embrace

I'm in love
Lord take all of me

I'm in love
My lover set me free

I'm in love
His name is Elohim

I'm in love
With His Majesty

I'm in love
He's brooding over me

So with my hands
out stretched

I'll sing out loud
I'm in Love…..

Song of Solomon 2:1-4

I am the rose of Sharon, and the lily of the valleys. As the lily among thorns, so is My love among the daughters. As the apple tree among the trees of the wood, so is My beloved among the sons. I sat down under His shadow with great delight, and His fruit was sweet to my taste. He brought me to the banqueting house, and His banner over me was love.

STOW AWAY BABY

Stow away baby
Please give me time

Stow away baby
The choice wasn't mine

Stow away baby
Doesn't have my eyes

Stow away baby
Returns my cry

Hands cold, with an icy bite
Colligated my fear, I didn't fight

No face, no soul, a horrendous stench
Why me, why now, it made no sense

Salty rain, became dew for my face
My heart dared time, to a silent race

My soul was quailed, nothing was left
Just the bitter taste, of an evil theft

Stow away baby
Alive and free

Stow away baby
Was left for me

Stow away baby
Renew my soul

Stow away baby
Will never be told......

John 10:9-11

For I am the door: by Me if any man enter in, he shall be saved, and shall go in and out, and find pasture. The thief cometh not, but for to steal, and to kill, and to destroy: I am come that they might have life, and that they might have it more abundantly. I am the good shepherd: the good shepherd giveth his life for the sheep.

HOLY SPIRIT REIGN OVER ME

TALKING, SUGGESTING
LAUNDERING
MY
HEART

NO GOOD THING
DWELLS IN THE FLESH
JUST WATCH
I'M GONNA PASS THIS TEST

FATHER, SON,
AND HOLY SPIRIT
I PRAISE MY GOD
ETERNITY

Holy Spirt Reign Over Me

BE QUIET
I'M TRYING
NOT TO
THINK

STOP!
DON'T ANYBODY MOVE
I HEAR THE SOUND
OF MY BREAKTROUGH

TOO MANY
VOICES
AND THEY
DON'T AGREE

TRUST IN THE LORD
TAKE REFUGE
MEDITATE THE WORD
AND LIVE

HOLY SPIRIT
REIGN
OVER
ME

DEATH
WHERE IS YOUR STING
I SOAR
ON EAGLE WINGS

SHHHHHHH!
BE QUIET FLESH
JUST WATCH
I'M GONNA PASS THIS TEST

SHHHHHHH! STOP!
DON'T ANYBODY MOVE
I HEAR THE VOICE OF VICTROY
IT'S GOD! HE'S EMPOWERED ME

AND NOW!
I ADDRESS THE MIND
"STAND DOWN"
THOUGHTS COME IN LINE

TO RULE MY FLESH
STAND MY GROUND
I'M FREE
I REFUSE TO BE BOUND

Luke 11:9-13

And I say unto you, Ask, and it shall be given you; seek, and ye shall find; knock, and it shall be opened unto you. For every one that asketh receiveth; and he that seeketh findeth, and to him that knocketh it shall be opened. If a son shall ask bread of any of you that is a father, will he give him a stone? Or if he ask a fish, will he for a fish give him a serpent? Or if he shall ask an egg, will he offer him a scorpion? If ye then, being evil, know how to give good gifts unto your children: how much more shall your heavenly Father give the Holy Spirit to them that ask Him?

THE BROKEN HOUSE

Everything Gone
The House Deplete
My Heart
Feels
Bitter Sweet

Looking At The Rooms
That Used To Be Mine
Makes The Move
Such A Crime

Unable To Touch
Any Of The Past
Slowly
I Put
On My Mask

Turn My Back
Preparing To Leave
Willing Myself
Not To Grieve

Once There Was
Laughter And Joy
Now What's Left
A Few Broken Toys

Stepping Out
Into
The Sunshine
Lord Something Wonderful
Came To Mind

That Moving On
Is Not A Loss
And Change Does
Have A Cost

See I Remember All The Changes
I Went Through
Like When All Of My Bills
Were Over Due, It Was You
Who Said Shhhhh, Peace

I'm Looking Back To When
I Didn't Even Have A Home
And I was Raising Both My Boys
All Alone, I Heard Shhhh, Peace

Then The Night My Car Had Given
Up And Died
Fear Came To Overwhelm Me And
I Had To Cry, I Heard Shhhh, Peace

And The Day The Sun Shined
Down On My Face And I Thought
My Life Was Nothing
But A Total Waste
He Said, Shhhh, Peace

See I Know That I Can Make It
Cause I'm Not Alone
I Know My House Will Be
A Happy Home
Because Of Peace

I Have Never Had A Friend
Who Compared To You
Lord You Kept Loving Me
When I Turned From You
I Have Peace

I'll Never Let You Go Again
I'm Never Giving You Up
Your Love and Understanding
Is Worth That Much
I Have Peace

So They Can Say That I am Crazy
They Can Call Me Insane
They Can Stick Any Label
Under My Name
I Have Peace

Now I Look Unto Heaven
Giving You All the Praise
Cause You Were The One
Who Helped Me Mend My Ways
I Have Peace

Lord Hold Me In Your Arms
Don't Ever Let Me Go
You Are The Best Friend
That I have ever known
I Have Peace

Father You're my hiding place
I am safe

My strength and shield
I am healed

My joy and laughter
My only Master

You Are my Fleece
I have Peace!

Philippians 4:4-7

Rejoice in the Lord always: and again I say, Rejoice. Let your moderation be known unto all men. The Lord is at hand. Be careful for nothing; but in everything by prayer and supplication with thanksgiving let your requests be made known unto God. And the peace of God, which passeth all understanding, shall keep your hearts and minds through Christ Jesus.

RESTORED

A falling leaf
Is what I am
Gently falling down

A falling leaf
Is what I am
Both eyes on the ground

A falling leaf
Is what I am
Holding back the pain

A falling leaf
Is what I am
Descending all alone

A falling leaf
Is what I am
Searching for a home

A fallen leaf
Is what I am
Covered by the dirt

A fallen leaf
Is what I am
Enveloped by the hurt

A fallen leaf
Is what I am
That drifted from above

A fallen leaf
Is what I am
That couldn't find love

Until Jesus arrived
And gathered the leaf
Into nail scared hands

His presence creating
A tranquil silence
He attends to the leaf

Jesus hears nothing else
Jesus sees nothing else
Only the broken leaf

Gentle fingers
Brush away dirt
And debris

His words of affection
Heal old scars and
Offer new life

He never departs
But graphs me into Himself
The tree of righteousness

I am a fallen leaf
Who received
A second chance

I am a fallen leaf
Healed
By God

I am a fallen leaf
Cleansed by the blood
I am a fallen leaf, Restored

Revelation 21:3-5

And I heard a great voice out of heaven saying, Behold, the tabernacle of God is with men, and He will dwell with them, and they shall be His people, and God Himself shall be with them and be their God. And God shall wipe away all tears from their eyes; and there shall be no more death, neither sorrow, nor crying, neither shall there be any more pain: for the former things are passed away. And He that sat upon the throne said, Behold, I make all things new. And He said unto me, Write: for these words are true and faithful.

MY TRUEST FRIEND

MY TRUEST FRIEND
IS NOT MAN
NOR WOMAN
BUT MY GOD

YOU SEE I SEARCHED FOR A FRIEND
WHO WOULD DRY MY TEARS
SOMEONE WHO COULD HELP ME
OVERCOME MY FEARS

A FRIEND
WITH WHOM I COULD RELAX
A FRIEND I COULD LOVE
HOLDING NOTHING BACK

A FRIEND WHO DIDN'T
BRING UP MY PAST
ONE WHO WANTED ME
TO TAKE OFF MY MASK

I WANTED A FRIEND
WHO LIKED GOING ON TRIPS
TO WASHINGTON, NEW YORK
I WANTED FELLOWSHIP

I WANTED A FRIEND
I COULD LOVE AND SUPPORT
ONE WHO COULD FORGIVE
WHEN I FELL SHORT

I WANTED SOMEONE
WHO WOULD SPEAK THEIR MIND
ESPECIALLY WHEN I
SPOKE OUT OF LINE

I WANTED A FRIEND
WHO WOULD NOT RUN AND HIDE
BUT ONE WHO WOULD FIGHT
STANDING BY MY SIDE

I SEARCHED FOR A FRIEND
WHO COULD BELIEVE
THAT I WAS NOT HOLDING
CARDS UP MY SLEEVE

AT LAST I'VE COME
TO THE END OF MY QUEST
NOW I CAN SAY
THAT MY HEART IS AT REST

I WAS SEARCHING FOR SOMEONE
TO CALL FRIEND
MY SEARCH ENDED
WHERE IT ALL BEGAN

WHERE THEY SPREAD HIS ARMS
AND NAILED HIS FEET
CROWNED HIS HEAD
WITH THORNS OF GRIEF

THEY CURSED HIS NAME
REJECTED HIS LOVE
AND HE SUBMITTED
LIKE A HELPLESS DOVE

HE ONCE SPOKE THESE WORDS
I CALL YOU FRIEND
KNOWING HE WOULD BE
MURDERED FOR MY SIN

I KNOW OF NO MAN
WHO WOULD DO WHAT HE DID
HE LAID DOWN HIS LIFE
FOR AN UNWORTHY FRIEND

I LOVE GOD SO MUCH
HE ENDED MY SEARCH
MY TRUEST FRIEND JESUS
HE DIED FOR THE CHURCH.....

Romans 5:6-8

While we were yet in weakness [powerless to help ourselves], at the fitting time Christ died for (in behalf of) the ungodly.   Now it is an extraordinary thing for one to give his life even for an upright man, though perhaps for a noble and lovable and generous benefactor someone might even dare to die.   But God shows and clearly proves His [own] love for us by the fact that while we were still sinners, Christ (the Messiah, the Anointed One) died for us.
[Amp]

WE ARE HER

Having fun with my sister
Jumping rope
Hopscotch
Laughing in the rain

Making pies
Baking cookies
Everyday
Being trained

Trained by
Ma
Oh how I miss
Those days

When trust was free
Laughter was pure
And fear
never came

But seasons have to change
No more jump rope
No more hopscotch
No more laughing in the rain

I see sister all alone
Bearing shame
Hiding pain
Now crying in the rain

Too many lies from men
Women betrayed her too
Why did I laugh
Instead of helping you

Ma would say
If one is weak
The other
Should lift her head

But when my sister's
Load was heavy
I shrugged
Turning away instead

But now I feel
So heavy
My heart
Filled with dread

So I spoke to Ma
About it
And this
Is what she said

How would YOU want
To be treated
If that pain
Was living in you

What if YOU kept
Making mistakes
And you didn't
Know what to do

What if
It was YOU
No one
Understood

Would YOU laugh
Would YOU rejoice
Would YOU embrace
Sisterhood?

Ma You sound like Granma
And sweetheart
You sound
Like me

When I was young and foolish
and didn't operate in love
Granma was the one
Who showed me what I was

But Ma you're so smart
So gentle
And always
Kind

Sweetie
Looks can be deceiving
And lies
Charm will hide

But Honey, Jesus
He changed me
He enlarged
My heart

To embrace
All my sisters
And no longer
Tear them apart

I've learned
Not to assume
Too much
About their pain

But to value them
And love them
And see the best
That they can be

I also learned
Their sins were not
Revealed for me
To share

But to lay before
the throne
And cover my sister
In prayer

Oh Ma
I'm so guilty
I just didn't
Know

But I'm CHANGING
I WON'T stay the same
Sister will have ME
I'll shield her from the rain

We'll laugh again
Dance again
I'll learn to be
Her friend

I'll lift her head up high
Encourage her
Even carry her
And she'll never be alone

Honey, sisters are like a puzzle
Alone were just a piece
But when we are all connected
You see our unity

Our different shapes and sizes
Our different anointings too
Unfold a beautiful picture
As a puzzle is meant to do

Unified were strong
And unified were bold
Together we can love
This world grown cold

Granma was quietly smiling
Observing her ministry
She now in her daughter
And my mother now in me

I didn't completely understand
It all seemed like a blur
Then suddenly I realized
"We are her"

2 Timothy 1:1-5

Paul, an apostle (special messenger) of Christ Jesus by the will of God, according to the promise of life that is in Christ Jesus, to Timothy, [my] beloved child: Grace (favor and spiritual blessing), mercy, and [heart] peace from God the Father and Christ Jesus our Lord! I thank God whom I worship with a pure conscience, in the spirit of my fathers, when without ceasing I remember you night and day in my prayers, and when, as I recall your tears, I yearn to see you so that I may be filled with joy. I am calling up memories of your sincere and unqualified faith (the leaning of your entire personality on God in Christ in absolute trust and confidence in His power, wisdom, and goodness), [a faith] that first lived permanently in [the heart of] your grandmother Lois and your mother Eunice and now, I am [fully] persuaded, [dwells] in you also. [Amp]

God's Promises are True

I know
That you don't
Cherish me
And that really hurts

But, Its o.k.
I'll be o.k.
because
God got me

I wanted
so bad
For you to be
True

Because I wanted someone
Who like me
Was loyal,
Faithful and true

Your heart
Not mine
Your love
Not mine

Just a mirage
That I created
In my
Mind

Thoughts of you
Now fill my mind
With grief, regret
And sorrow

While my heart
Bleeds and bleeds
From all your lies
And betrayals

My eyes search your face
My ears search your words
My hope search your promises
For a small hint of character:

Integrity, Love,
Regret, Loyalty
Repentance
Any positive change

But still
I am met
With more of
Your little clever lies

How do I leave
How do I start again
How do I
Let go

My heart is lost
My heart is broken
My heart
So Deceived

I was promised
Love, Romance, Laughter
Protection and Affection; but I got
Only cunning smiles and lies

My heart loves him
But I need love too
My heart held lovingly
Deep within his chest

I need to feel special
I need to matter
Not just enough
To say that you did

I need genuine love
Sensual touch
And YOUR words
Of love

My hearts becoming hollow
Struggling to love
Grasping
For hope

Dream Breaker
Why
Win my heart
Then crush it

Yet
I believe that
God is True
And He's still in love with you

So I'll keep confessing:
God will redeem, God will heal
God will deliver
God will restore our love

Then suddenly!
God stirred up the man
My husband hid
From me

I see the light
Of truth again
Shinning from
His eyes

My husband is now redeemed
Our love blossomed too
Our Marriage is renewed
Because God's Promises are True

Jeremiah 3:14-15

Only acknowledge thine iniquity, that thou hast transgressed against the Lord thy God, and hast scattered thy ways to the strangers under every green tree, and ye have not obeyed my voice, saith the Lord. Turn, O backsliding children, saith the Lord; for I am married unto you: and I will take you one of a city, and two of a family, and I will bring you to Zion: And I will give you pastors according to mine heart, which shall feed you with knowledge and understanding.

FORGIVENESS

Forgive the ones
Who hurt me
Deserted me
Who left me for dead

How? Why?
What's in it for me?
Move on, let it go
No one wants to know

My heart plastered
Hiding gnashes and scares
Layer upon layer
Of fear grown hard

It hurts so bad
To hear what I must do
It hurts when they say
I must forgive you

Your weakness
Encircling, devouring me
You! So oblivious
Smiling with glee

When I think of letting go
Forgiving all you've done
I'm silenced by thoughts
That your evil has won

Can forgiveness birth
Hope for change
Or just mask
Unbearable pain

God says in His Word
Forgiving you heals me
Yet I do not sense
This victory

I find no comfort
In what I feel
I need to find
Forgiveness that heals

I am unlearned
I am untaught
The forgiveness I offered
It was not

I am immature
Until I learn to forgive
I am dead
I can not live

Lord teach me what
Forgiveness is not
Lord teach me to forgive
From my heart...

Matthew 6:12-14

And forgive us our debts, as we also have forgiven (left, remitted, and let go of the debts, and have given up resentment against) our debtors. And lead (bring) us not into temptation, but deliver us from the evil one. For Yours is the kingdom and the power and the glory forever. Amen. For if you forgive people their trespasses (their reckless and willful sins, leaving them, letting them go, and giving up resentment), your heavenly Father will also forgive you. [Amp]

WHOM DO YOU SERVE?

They say that Christmas
Is all about "My Birth"
Love, joy
And peace on earth

Yet year after year
I watch the same display
As my birthday becomes
Idolatry Day

You say what idols
We believe in God
Though your homes are
Decorated for santa clause

A toy can't replace
MY gift of love
Before santa existed
I already was

I see smiles on faces
With hearts that are grieving
You've pulled out masks
For this thirty day season

You laugh very loud
Everywhere you go
But sweetheart the truth
Is beginning to show

Year after year
You would not choose me
You chose santa clause
And his make believe glee

You told your children
"Leave santa cookies and milk"
While you wrapped precious
Gifts Of satin or silk

Not once did you say,
"Kids, Jesus died for you
And He's why I'm buying
These gifts for you"

You never did tell them
About my birth
And that's the part
That really, really hurts

When you were in pain
You cried my name
And as you know
I quickly came

So on the day
That belongs to me
Don't join unbelievers
In their false melee

But remember the baby
Who was born to you
With a red beating heart
Yes! I can hurt too

And when My birthday
Begins to draw nigh
Remember your God
Can also cry

All I am really
Trying to say
Exalt Me on Christmas
It's MY birthday!

Love….King Jesus

Luke 2:10-14

And the angel said unto them, Fear not: for behold, I bring you good tidings of great joy, which shall be to all people. For unto you is born this day in the city of David a Saviour, which is Christ the Lord. And this shall be a sign unto you; Ye shall find the babe wrapped in swaddling clothes, lying in a manger. And suddenly there was with the angel a multitude of the heavenly host praising God, and saying, Glory to God in the highest, and on earth peace, good will towards men.

THE BLOOD

HA, HA, HA
YOU LAUGHED GLEEFULLY
WHEN I SAID
ONE DAY I WOULD BE FREE

BECAUSE MY POWERFUL WILL
AND MY SET DETERMINATION
TURNED UGLY TO GOD
AND BECAME An ABOMINATION

BUT I WOULDN'T BE MOVED
I STAYED TO FIGHT
BECAUSE I KNEW
I HAD TO WALK RIGHT

THERE WAS NO QUESTION
NO DEBATE OR DOUBT
MY GOD CAST
ALL THOSE DEMONS OUT

NEVER AGAIN COULD I
COME AND GO
BECAUSE GO LET ME KNOW
THAT HE RUNS THE SHOW

I HAD TURNED AWAY
FROM MY WICKED WAYS
AND GOD SAID TO ME
BLESSED BE YOUR DAYS

BUT SILLY, FOOLISH PEOPLE
TRIED TO HURT ME
BECAUSE THEY COULDN'T SEE
THAT GOD HAD SET ME FREE

THOUGH I SLIPPED FOR A MOMENT
YES I FELL
BUT I KNEW I WASN'T FACING
THE GATES OF HELL

YOU SEE A LONG TIME AGO
DOWN ON CALVARY
A WONDERFUL MAN
PAID A DEBT FOR ME

I DON'T KNOW WHY HE DID IT
I SHOULD BE DEAD
BUT HE CHOSE
TO BOW HIS HEAD

SO NOW WHY WOULD THE DEVIL
CLAIM THAT I WAS HIS WIFE
WHEN HE NEVER MOVED A FINGER
TO SAVE MY LIFE

IT WAS THE TRINTY
ONE, TWO, THREE
THEY WERE THE ONE'S
WHO REACHED OUT TO SAVE ME

LET ME TELL YOU HOW THEY DID IT
STARTING WITH NUMBER ONE
GOD THE FATHER
SENT DOWN HIS ONLY SON

MOVING RIGHT ALONG
ON TO NUMBER TWO
JESUS THE CHRIST
TOLD ME WHAT TO DO

HE SAID PRAY TO ME
TRUST IN ME
AND I GUARANTEE
YOU'LL BELONG TO ME

NOW I KNOW THAT YOU'RE WONDERING
WHAT ABOUT THREE
BECAUSE IT SOUNDS LIKE
YOU'VE BEEN SET FREE

WELL NUMBER THREE'S SORT OF SPECIAL	THE BLOOD
CAUSE YOU'VE GOT TO SHARE IT	THE
HE WAS SENT FROM JESUS CHRIST	DOVE
HOLY SPIRIT	THE RAM IN THE BUSH
HOLY SPIRIT WAS SENT	THE BLOOD
FOR YOU	THE
AND FOR ME	LOVE
COMFORTER, AFTER WE BECAME FREE	THE SACRIFICIAL GIFT
NOW IF YOU'RE THINKING IN YOUR HEAD	THE BLOOD
I'M ALREADY FREE	THE
TAKE MY ADVICE	CROSS
AND LISTEN TO ME	CHRIST PAID THE COST
DON'T LET THE DEVIL TELL YOU	THE BLOOD
THAT YOU'RE ALL SET	THE
BECAUSE A TRIALS GONNA COME	TREE
THAT YOU'VE NEVER MET	HE SET US FREE
NOW WHEN YOU MEET THAT TRIAL	THE
HERE'S WHAT YOU SHOULD DO	BLOOD
GATHER YOUR ARMOR	THE NARROW WAY
UNTO YOU	LO, I AM WITH YOU ALWAYS
STAND YOUR GROUND	AND I'LL BE BACK
LOOK SATAN IN THE EYE	TO MAKE MY SEARCH
SAY SATAN, YOUR GONNA DIE	SO PLEASE
AND I HAVE MY REASONS WHY	DON'T FORSAKE MY CHURCH!

Colossians 1:12:14

Giving thanks unto the Father, which hath made us meet
to be partakers of the inheritance of the saints in light:
Who hath delivered us from the power of darkness, and
hath translated us into the kingdom of his dear son:
In whom we have redemption through His blood,
even the forgiveness of sins.

LOYALTY

Loyalty is as
A breath of fresh air
On a brisk wintry day

It is clean
And unhindered
It is fresh And inviting

It offers life
A renewal
Of hope

Loyalty emanates
Such power
Like the splendorous

Magnificent roar
Of the rushing
Niagara falls

A glorious beauty
Demanding respect
Honor and awe

Uncontrolled and fierce
Yet unmovable
And free

Loyalty
is positioned
On solid ground

with a sure foundation
No faltering
No sway

This is the essence
This is the way
This is the power of loyalty

Ruth 1:8-17

And Naomi said unto her two daughters in law, Go, return each to her mother's house: the Lord deal kindly with you, as ye have dealt with the dead, and with me. The Lord grant you that you may find rest, each of you in the house of her husband. Then she kissed them; and they lift up their voice, and wept. And they said unto her, Surely we will return with thee unto thy people. And Naomi said, turn again, my daughters: why will you go with me? Are there yet any more sons in my womb, that they may be your husbands? Turn again, my daughters, go your way; for I am too old to have a husband. If I should say, I have hope, if I should have a husband also tonight, and should also bear sons; Would ye tarry for them till they were grown? Would ye stay for them from having husbands? Nay, my daughters; for it grieveth me much for your sakes that the hand of the Lord is gone out against me. And they lift up their voice, and wept again: and Orpah kissed her mother in law; but Ruth clave unto her. And she said, Behold, thy sister in law is gone back unto her people, and unto her gods: return thou after thy sister in law. And Ruth said, Urge me not to leave thee, or to return from following after thee: for whither thou goest, I will go; and where thou lodgest, I will lodge: thy people shall be my people, and thy God my God: Where thou diest, will I die, and there will I be buried: the Lord do so to me, and more also if anything but death part thee and me.

THE TRUE COLOR OF LOVE

Like the blood that flowed through our Saviors veins
Love is warm

Like the Blood that trailed down our Saviors face
Love has a path

Like the Blood that ran down our Saviors side
Love is ever flowing

Like the blood of our Savior that stained the ground
Love leaves its mark

Like the Blood that was given to cover all sin
Love is unselfish

Like the Blood that saved our broken lives
Love is not you

Love is not me
Love is our Jesus, Eternity

Jesus' Blood
The true color of love

Isaiah 53:3-5

He is despised and rejected of men; a man of sorrows, and acquainted with grief: and we hid as it were our faces from him; he was despised, and we esteemed him not. Surely he hath borne our griefs, and carried our sorrows: yet we did esteem him stricken, smitten of god, and afflicted. But he was wounded for our transgressions, he was bruised for our iniquities: the chastisement of our peace was upon him; and with his stripes we are healed.

VICTORIOUS ME

Simply said
Simply put
No one will
Remove my foot

Head held high
Refusing to quit
Oh look at
Victorious Me

Never weak
I work & play hard
While leaning
On my God

My Savior, My King
My Healer
Oh look at
Victorious Me

I will see
no demise
I have the
upper hand

My laughter
And joy
Are my prize
I walk among the wise

Smiling inside and out
Enjoying all I see
Oh look at
Victorious Me

Transforming who I am
Renewing my inner man
I Speak words of life
I refuse to live in strife

Hoping
Receiving
Trusting
Believing

I embrace life
I live to be free
I am victorious
I am victorious me

Isaiah 1:11-12

Therefore the redeemed of the Lord shall return, and come with singing unto Zion; and everlasting joy shall be upon their head: they shall obtain gladness and joy; and sorrow and mourning shall flee away. I, even I, am He that comforteth you: who art thou, that thou shouldest be afraid of a man that shall die, and of the son of man which shall be made as grass;

True Love

TRUE LOVE
IS LIKE
A SOFT SILKY
WHITE FLOWER

SOLITARY
AND ALONE
BUT SO ELEGANT
AND BEAUTIFUL

GROWING IN
AN OPEN FIELD
BASKING IN THE
MOONS RAYS

HIDDEN BY THE MASK
OF NIGHT
YET EXPOSED
TO EVERYONE

TRUE LOVE
PATIENTLY ENJOYS
THE TICKING
HANDS OF TIME

THE SOFT FLOWER
LAVISHES THE EARTH
THAT IS DRAWING HER
CLOSER TO THE SUN

JUST AS TRUE LOVE
LURES TWO LOVERS
INTO A DANCE CALLED
"CHERISH ME"

HE OFFERS HIS HAND,
SHE ACCEPTS
SHE STEPS INTO
HIS EMBRACE

THEIR EYES LOCK
IN AGREEMENT AND
THEY BEGIN THE DANCE
"CHERISH ME"

LIKE THE BEAUTIFUL
SILKY WHITE FLOWER
CARESSED
BY THE BREEZE

FED BY
THE RAIN
AND TESTED
BY STORMS

TRUE LOVE
WILL REMAIN
WHEN THE MUSIC
CAN'T BE HEARD

TRUE LOVE
WILL KEEP DANCING
ENDURING THE RAIN
DEFYING THE STORM

EXPECTING TO SEE
TO FEEL, TO TOUCH
EXPECTING TO HEAR
THEIR MUSIC AGAIN

TRUE LOVE
WILL RECALL
THAT
FIRST DANCE

CALLED, "CHERISH ME"
YES, TRUE LOVE
WILL
REMEMBER

THE FIRST TOUCH
THE FIRST KISS
THE FIRST PROMISE
THE FIRST EMBRACE

LIKE THE SOFT
SILKY WHITE FLOWER
LOVINGLY AWAITED
THE SUNS EMBRACE

AFTER THE WINDS
AFTER THE CONFUSION
AFTER THE STORM
THE FLOWER REMAINED

ONLY TRUE LOVE
CAN DANCE IN THE RAIN
ONLY TRUE LOVE CAN
ENDURE THE PAIN

ONLY TRUE LOVE
CAN TRULY BE FREE
ONLY TRUE LOVE
CAN CHERISH ME

TRUE LOVE.......

1 Corinthians 13:4-7

Love endures long and is patient and kind; love never is envious nor boils over with jealousy, is not boastful or vainglorious, does not display itself haughtily. It is not conceited (arrogant and inflated with pride); it is not rude (unmannerly) and does not act unbecomingly. Love (God's love in us) does not insist on its own rights or its own way, for it is not self-seeking; it is not touchy or fretful or resentful; it takes no account of the evil done to it [it pays no attention to a suffered wrong]. It does not rejoice at injustice and unrighteousness, but rejoices when right and truth prevail. Love bears up under anything and everything that comes, is ever ready to believe the best of every person, its hopes are fadeless under all circumstances, and it endures everything [without weakening]. [Amp]

WHY

I PROMISED THE LORD
I WOULD SIN NO MORE
BUT I NEVER KNEW
WHAT THE FUTURE HELD
IN STORE

I PROMISED THE LORD
I WOULD NOT GO ASTRAY
BUT I NEVER KNEW
I WAS STILL FINDING MY WAY

I PROMISED THE LORD
I WOULD NOT LIVE A LIE
BUT STILL MY ACTIONS
CAUSED ME TO SIGH

THE LORD HEARD EVERY
PROMISE
THAT I MADE
AND HE ALSO WATCHED
EACH ONE FADE

I KNELT DOWN BESIDE MY BED
I TOLD THE LORD
I WAS WRONG & NEXT TIME
I WOULD BE MORE STRONG

I TOLD HIM THAT I
HAD ANALYZED MY LIFE
& I KNEW THE OLD MAN
WAS CAUSING THIS STRIFE

I ENDED THE PRAYER
WITH AMEN
SOON AFTER
I SINNED AGAIN

I NEVER TOOK THE TIME
TO REPENT & AS THE YEARS
CAME AND WENT
I TOOK FOR GRANTED
WHAT MY SALVATION MEANT

THEN ONE DAY
IT ALL CAME TO AN END
AND I DESPERATELY CRIED OUT
FOR JESUS MY FRIEND

MY CRY ECHOED INTO THE NIGHT
AS I SEARCHED FOR LIGHT
THEN I CAUGHT A GLIMPSE
OF A SHIMMER OF WHITE

I FELT SOMEONE BY MY SIDE
AND ALL THEY WISPHERED
TO ME WAS "WHY"
AT THAT MOMENT
I BEGAN TO CRY

BECAUSE I KNEW
THAT I WOULD DIE
SOON THE LORD
MADE MY DEATH CLEAR

AND THESE
WERE THE LAST
WORDS
THAT I COULD HEAR

YOU REJECTED MY SON
AND HARDENED YOUR HEART
DEPART FROM ME
FOR I KNOW YOU NOT…..

Matthew 7:21-23

Not every one that saith unto me, Lord, Lord, shall enter into the kingdom of heaven; but he that doeth the will of my Father which is in heaven. Many will say to me in that day, Lord, Lord, have we not prophesied in thy name? And in thy name done many wonderful works? And then will I profess unto them, I never knew you: depart from me, ye that work iniquity (act wickedly, disregarding my commands).

THE STORY THAT I WRITE

The story that I write
Is about a face dried by tears
Yet the tears could not
Wash away the pain and fears

I write about two brown eyes
Blood red from crying
Because they saw a life
Slowly dying

I write about a mind
Throbbing with confusion
From living a life
Of truth and illusion

I write of a heart
Hurt and in pain
Beating yet knowing
The rhythm is in vain

I write of two black hands
Grasping the rock
As the wind and rain
Tear at her frock

I write of two black feet
Standing their ground
As the owner wonders
Where peace can be found

Warm dark skin
Dried by heat
A display of how life
Can be bittersweet

A young woman
Bending with strain
Withstanding the pressure
Of all of life's pain

I write of the beginning
and end of a cry
I write of a baby
who never knew why

I write of a choice
that was made
I write of a memory
that will not fade......

Isaiah 1:18-20

Come now, and let us reason together, saith the Lord: though your sins be as scarlet, they shall be as white as snow; though they be red like crimson, they shall be as wool.

HAPPY NEW YEAR

May your Christmas be filled
with laughter and cheer
As you prepare for another new year

May your family be healthy
And prospering too
As you prepare to see another year through

May your Christmas produce
Memories of bliss
Like a soft warm summers kiss

I wish you the best
For the months to come
I hope every obstacle you'll overcome

With warm wishes
And kind thoughts too
I hope this New Year brings the best to you!

Merry Christmas & Happy New Year!

Isaiah 43:18-19

Remember ye not the former things, neither consider the things of old. Behold, I will do a new thing; now it shall spring forth; shall ye not know it? I will even make a way in the wilderness, and rivers in the desert.

MALACHI 3:10

Faithful kind
Dependable and true
Prove me
You know what to do

Tithe
Pray
Seek my face
Prove me
Hallow My Name

Walk by faith
Not by sight
Prove me
And I'll honor you

I'm the Most High God
Dependable and true
Love me
Heaven will open to you

Grasp My Word
Eat it day and night
Prove me
And I'll favor you

After I promote you
Bring glory to Me
Return
And worship Me

Meditate My Word
Meditate My Name
Prove Me
I'll never change

Prove Me....and reign!

Malachi 3:10

Bring ye all the tithes into the storehouse, that there may be meat in mine house, And prove me (test me) now herewith, saith the Lord of hosts, if I will not open you the windows of heaven, and pour you out a blessing, that there shall not be room enough to receive it.

THE LORD GOD CAN DO ANYTHING

Her heart was heavy
Head hung low
She prayed her troubles
Wouldn't show

She slowly sighed
And leaned back on the door
Gazed at her feet
That were swollen and sore

Tired brown eyes
Scaled four flights of stairs
As she quietly willed
I'm already there

She took one step
And then another
She sighed and whispered
We can make it together

She held tight to the banister
And continued to climb
As the days conversations
Raced through her mind

THE FIRST PERSON SAID:

It does not matter
If your rent is due
I'm running a business
I want my money too!

AND ANOTHER SAID:

Ma'am your train is at
Gate number eight
But I'm sorry to inform you
You're one minute too late

SOMEONE ELSE STATED:

I know that we promised
You'd work here till June
But unfortunately
You're terminated at noon

THE LAST PERSON EXPLAINED:

Ma'am you've missed
Your appointment
It was scheduled for yesterday
Are you and baby doing okay

Then she remembered
Her husband's words
"It's o.k." Stuff like this
Happens everyday

She stopped for a moment
Closed her eyes
And said LORD
I will not cry

She felt the movement
Within her womb
A gentle reminder
That the child would come soon

The climb continued
Up the steps
Control was lost
The young woman wept

Descending down
She slid to the floor
The woman's mind
Couldn't bear anymore

All is quiet
All is still
Her mind and body
Lost their will

Gently her hair
Was caressed by a breeze
As a voice softly said
I'll supply your needs

The voice continued
Your Lord is here
I heard you cry
And I counted each tear

I know of the pain
You're going through
But I have so much more
In store for you

The woman smiled
At the familiar touch
She said "Lord, I am tired
Yet, I love you so much"

The voice spoke again
Get up and live
Or have you forgotten
Who the Lord Your God is

Some call me Jesus
Some call me Christ
I was called King
Of the Israelites

I am Elohim
Or Elshadi
Holy, Holy, Holy
Am also I

I — Am God
Ruler of all
King of the Jews
I was also called

My name is
I Am that I Am
Yet still some call me
The Sacrificial Lamb

The woman stood up
And began to sing
Lord my God
You can do anything

These set backs
Can not last
In fact I declare
They're already past

My Lord, My Lord
My Holy, Holy King
To You My God
I worship and sing

The woman worshipped
As she walked away
Praising the God
Who can do anything

Many years later
You could still hear her sing
The Lord my God
Can do anything!

Exodus 14:13-14

Is not this the word that we did tell thee in Egypt, saying, Let us alone, that we may serve the Egyptians? For it had been better for us to serve the Egyptians, than that we should die in the wilderness. And Moses said unto the people, fear ye not, stand still, and see the salvation of the Lord, which He will shew to you today: for the Egyptians whom ye have seen today, ye shall see them again no more for ever. The Lord shall fight for you, and ye shall hold your peace.

I PROMISE

Where life will take us
I do not know
But I hope
We will continue to grow

I don't know if our home
Will be big or small
But I know you are
My all in all

I can't promise that
Our life will be grand
But by your side
I am going to stand

I can't promise
How many children we'll bear
But I can say
I will always be here

I can't promise you that
Our bank account will double
But I will be with you
Whenever there's trouble

I can't guarantee
There will never be strife
But my love, I offer you
my heart & my life

1 Corinthians 2:9

But as it is written, Eye hath not seen, nor ear heard, neither have entered into the Heart of man, the things which God hath prepared for them that love Him.

Index

- Oh How She Loved You
- You Can Always Come Home
- The Drop of A Tear
- Dear Mom & Dad
- May I Come In
- My Brothers
- Dear Heart
- I Belong To You
- I Am Royalty
- I Am Holy Spirit
- Black against Black
- Special Mother
- Our Love
- Open The Door
- Alive
- My Dearest Love
- My Lover
- A True Friend
- Choose To Be A Woman
- God's Bible on the Shelf
- A Lie
- Embrace
- My Son
- I Got Too Much Class
- This Couple is Blessed
- There's No Me, Without You
- The Worshiper
- The Secret
- Stow Away Baby
- Holy Spirit Reign Over Me
- The Broken House
- Restored
- My Truest Friend
- We Are Her
- Suddenly
- Forgiveness
- Whom Do You Serve
- The Blood
- Loyalty
- The True Color of Love
- Victorious Me
- True Love
- Why
- The Story That I Write
- Happy New Year
- Malachi 3:10
- The Lord God Can Do Anything
- I Promise

Created and Designed

By

Alva Williams

A product of L&A Williams
P.O. Box 7170
Hampton, VA 23666
www.lawilliams.org— lawilliams21@yahoo.com

www.ingramcontent.com/pod-product-compliance
Lightning Source LLC
Chambersburg PA
CBHW042321150426
43192CB00001B/12